VOICES FROM THE EARLY CHURCH

Study by Jodi Harris
Commentary by Guy Sayles and
Hardy Clemons

Free downloadable Teaching Guide for this study available at
NextSunday.com/teachingguides

NextSunday Resources
6316 Peake Road
Macon, Georgia 31210-3960
1-800-747-3016
©2021 by NextSunday Resources
All rights reserved.

TABLE OF CONTENTS

Voices from the Early Church

HOW TO USE THIS STUDY

NextSunday Resources Adult Bible Studies are designed to help adults study Scripture seriously within the context of the larger Christian tradition and, through that process, find their faith renewed, challenged, and strengthened. We study the Scriptures because we believe they affect our current lives in important ways. Each study contains the following three components:

Study Guide

Each study guide lesson is arranged in four movements:

Reflecting recalls a contemporary story, anecdote, example, or illustration to help us anticipate the session's relevance in our lives.

Remembering provides a frame of reference for the Scriptures.

Studying is centered on giving the biblical material in-depth attention while often surrounding it with helpful insights from theology, ethics, church history, and other areas.

Understanding helps us find relevant connections between our lives and the biblical message.

What About Me? provides brief statements that help unite life issues with the meaning of the biblical text.

Commentary

Each study guide lesson is accompanied by an additional, in-depth commentary on the biblical material. Written by a different author than the study guide, each commentary gives the opportunity for learners to approach the Scripture text from a separate but complementary viewpoint.

Teaching Guide

In addition to the provided study guide and commentary, *NextSunday Resources* also provides a *free* downloadable teaching guide, available at NextSunday.com. Each teaching guide gives the teacher tools for focusing on the content of each study guide lesson through additional commentary and Bible background information. Through teacher helps and teaching options, each teaching guide also provides substance for variety and choice in the preparation of each lesson.

NextSunday
Resources

STUDY INTRODUCTION

One of the challenges of written correspondence is saying all you want in as few words as possible. Sometimes the most meaningful and personal letters are the ones with only a few heartfelt words. The same is true for the New Testament letters we will explore in this unit.

Although short in length, Philemon, Titus, Jude, and 2 Timothy communicate large ideas. Their appeals to the early Christian church echo beyond the text and into our lives as Christians. In the next four sessions, we listen to voices from the early church that speak of transforming faith, complete commitment, outward actions, and persecution.

In Philemon, Paul confronts the church with a new way of thinking that ultimately transforms the whole community. Second Timothy speaks of commitment, even in a world of persecution. Not only does the author provide encouraging words for suffering, but he also challenges us to endure. Our third session from Titus focuses on the persecuted church in Crete. We will explore how this group of Christians relates to the community at large. Their public behavior is the focus of our attention. In Jude, persecution continues for the people of faith. "Scoffers" in the church were causing major divisions. The writer warns Christians about false teachers, and he gives them advice on how to deal with their brothers and sisters who have strayed from faith.

Although we can never understand the extent to which the community of faith faced persecution, the voices of the early church still speak to our own struggles and difficulties as we seek to follow God. Even more, their words summon us to respond. As we begin this journey, may we open our ears and be ready to listen for God's voice.

1

SPEAKING OF CHALLENGE

Philemon 8-16

Central Question

How is God calling us to change?

Scripture

Philemon 8-16 For this reason, though I am bold enough in Christ to command you to do your duty, 9 yet I would rather appeal to you on the basis of love—and I, Paul, do this as an old man, and now also as a prisoner of Christ Jesus. 10 I am appealing to you for my child, Onesimus, whose father I have become during my imprisonment. 11 Formerly he was useless to you, but now he is indeed useful both to you and to me. 12 I am sending him, that is, my own heart, back to you. 13 I wanted to keep him with me, so that he might be of service to me in your place during my imprisonment for the gospel; 14 but I preferred to do nothing without your consent, in order that your good deed might be voluntary and not something forced. 15 Perhaps this is the reason he was separated from you for a while, so that you might have him back forever, 16 no longer as a slave but more than a slave, a beloved brother—especially to me but how much more to you, both in the flesh and in the Lord..

Reflecting

When was the last time your church welcomed change? Most of us would admit that our congregations rarely yearn for change.

In most churches, change occurs slowly and usually with resistance. We are comfortable where we are.

While working as a minister of education, I occasionally had the delicate task of asking adult Sunday school classes to change rooms. This is one of the most dreaded tasks in Christian education. Sunday school classes tend to claim their space, and it is hard for them to let go. No matter how carefully and thoughtfully I made the request for a class to move to another room, each time I wondered if I should go home and pack my bags, thinking they would rather move *me* to another church than move their class down the hall. Thankfully, we can find humor in these experiences of church life. Moving out of our comfort zones is difficult, but our faith calls us to even greater challenges.

Paul challenged the church in Colossae to make a major adjustment. He was not asking this congregation to change Sunday school rooms. He was challenging them to make a difference in a slave's life, which would lead to change in the community itself. The situation in Colossae allows us to reflect on both personal and communal challenges. God can transform broken relationships, injustices in our communities, and divisions in our churches if we are willing to change and to be vessels of change. Are we open to the challenges this kind of faith demands? Are we ready to respond? Before we ask these questions, we must begin with the underlying question: Does our faith *really* make a difference?

Remembering

This session's Scripture text is the middle segment of Paul's letter to Philemon and to the church that met in Philemon's house. Paul opens with his usual greeting and then thanksgiving for the diligent work and genuine faith of this group of believers (vv. 1-7). Paul was obviously encouraged and pleased with the church's activity in the community: "I always thank my God because I hear of your love for all the saints and your faith toward the Lord Jesus" (vv. 4b-5). Paul

It was common for early church congregations to meet in the home of one of their members.

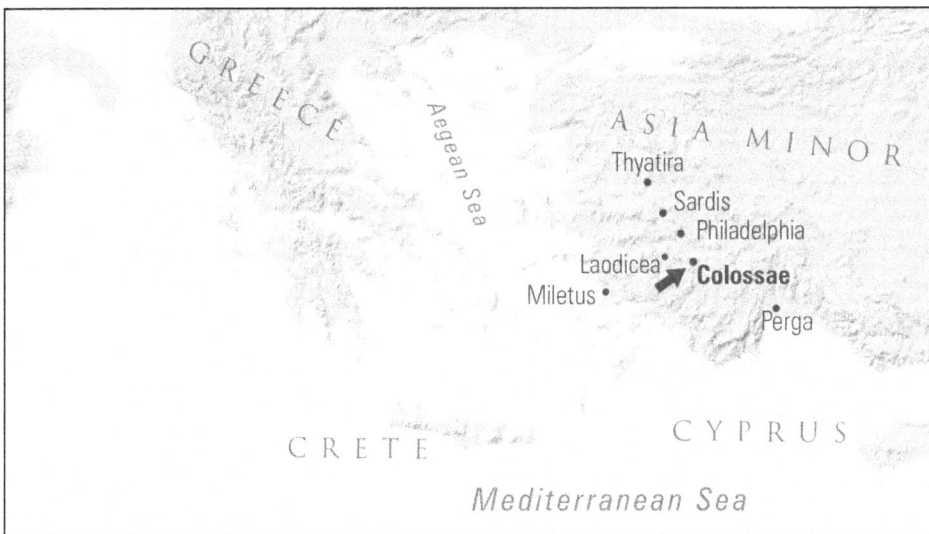

noticed their good work, but he knew the challenges that were ahead.

Colossae, one of the larger cities in the Lycus Valley of Asia Minor, had a mix of religious influence in Paul's time. Christianity was struggling to spread its message, as were Judaism and various mystery religions from the East and West. The environment was complex, with many different religions and philosophies infiltrating society. Consequently, it was difficult to distinguish between authentic Christianity and a Christian faith polluted with foreign worship practices. Paul fully intended to challenge this community to act as if their faith made a difference in how they lived.

Studying

Although imprisoned when he wrote this letter, readers can sense Paul's close connection to his original recipients. He addressed the letter to Philemon, the church that met in his house, and two other co-workers. Paul begins by acknowledging the love and encouragement he received from Philemon and the church (v. 7). He writes of their work in the name of Christ and thanks God for their faith. Above all, Paul emphasizes their love, or *agape*, the foundation for his appeal in the next verses (vv. 8-16).

Reading this brief letter, we realize that Paul was in the middle of a tense situation. Somehow, while in prison or traveling, Paul met Onesimus, one of Philemon's slaves. Onesimus had apparently run away from Philemon for reasons unknown to us. Whatever the reason, Onesimus had broken the law. It was risky for Paul to associate with Onesimus, much less consider him beneficial for spreading the gospel. Whereas Philemon and the larger community would have reprimanded and punished Onesimus for his wrongdoing, Paul challenged their ways and called them to respond with love and forgiveness.

Paul's appeal to the church on Onesimus's behalf is interesting. Paul could have exercised his apostolic authority to tell the church their duty as people of faith. Instead, he made his appeal based on love (vv. 8-9). In other words, Paul had the right to order Philemon to do the right thing, but he left the choice up to Philemon. Paul did not command or point fingers. His relationship with Philemon called for something different. He based his challenge in Christian love, hoping the church would embrace the decision to change and respond likewise. He knew the only way to generate true change was to allow the church to reach their own decision based on their understanding of reconciliation (v. 14).

The "parental" figure of speech Paul uses in reference to his relationship with Onesimus (v. 10) indicates that Onesimus had been transformed from a wandering slave to a beloved child of God. Paul points out that Onesimus would be more "useful" as a child in the Christian faith than he was as a slave. He would truly live up to his name Onesimus, which means *useful*.

Paul hesitated to send Onesimus back to Philemon because he had become his helper and companion for the sake of the gospel (v. 13). Yet Paul understood that he must return Onesimus to Philemon—not only because the law required it, but more importantly because Onesimus now belonged to the church. The church in Colossae would be forced to choose whether

Some suggest that Paul may have been hinting for Philemon to send Onesimus back to him on permanent loan, since Paul's imprisonment required that he have helpers to spread the gospel (Vinson, 633).

to accept him as a beloved brother in Christ or to punish him as a runaway slave.

Onesimus had changed and Paul called the church to change. Philemon and the community only knew Onesimus as a slave who broke the law and their trust. Paul challenged them to know Onesimus as a servant in the Lord and a brother in fellowship: "When Paul made his plea to Philemon to 'receive [Onesimus, now converted], back no longer as a slave but more than a slave, a beloved brother' (v. 16), it should be forcefully clear that Paul wanted Philemon to honor their new tie as Christians *above and beyond* any legal demands" (Felder, 900-901).

Understanding

While knowing the context and something of the original community is vital to understanding Paul's argument—after all, we are reading someone else's mail—the real meaning of this letter is found in a simple but profound claim: being Christian should affect how we act. Paul saw an opportunity for the believers at Colossae to *be* the church, but first they had to *change*, to be transformed.

To what change might God be calling your church?

The church in Colossae was thriving. Paul praised them on their encouraging and faithful work. By our standards, congregations might well model their ministry after churches like this one at Colossae. Yet, despite their achievements, they were missing an important part of their mission. Not only did Onesimus, one of their own, need acceptance, care, and spiritual nurture, but Philemon and his church needed evidence that they were the people to provide this care. Paul challenged the believers to offer Onesimus, a slave and a law-breaker, what the world would not— love and forgiveness. Paul knew such grace would allow the body of Christ to be transformed into the church God called it to be. We must not mistake this transformation as a small change. What Paul asked of Philemon and his congregation was radical. To move Onesimus from "slave" to "brother" in the eyes of the larger community presented a difficult choice for this church. The move would challenge other congregations, other Christians in the community, to do the same. The potential effect on the community was enormous.

The challenge for transformation continues. Unfortunately, many churches are struggling to *keep* people, so it is no wonder that we find it hard to *reach* people. In the process of "keeping," many congregations focus on meeting the needs of their members. While this is important, congregations must not lose sight of serving the rest of God's kingdom. Brokenness, injustice, and apathy are so prevalent and pervasive that we become calloused to the hurting world. Yet our calling as Christians is to confront injustices, to act out of love and forgiveness, and to offer a sanctuary of peace and refuge for hurting people. While the church must be a resting place for the weary, it must also be a place of transformation for the complacent. Cain Hope Felder notes, "Unlike Paul's setting, which was dominated by Rome's worldwide system of rule, our surroundings are smaller pockets of organized life within which our voices and votes and personal vision can have some impact" (901). Many hurting people are seeking sanctuary or refuge, but how many of these people do we find in *our* sanctuaries?

Congregations cannot afford to be naïve about the kind of change Paul's ministry represents. To embrace rather than restrict, to demand justice rather than status quo, to offer grace rather than judgment means challenging everyone around us to do the same. That kind of ministry is bold and prophetic.

Living out our faith is risky. Like the church in Colossae, we must always be open to how God might change us. We must remember that Paul's love for the church and for Onesimus motivated his appeal to Philemon. Out of Christlike love, we are given the strength and courage to make real changes within ourselves and within the world around us. We *can* make a difference if we are willing and responsive. The courage to be that kind of follower is uncommon but not unheard of, even today.

What About Me?

• *Where there is faith, there is challenge.* Being a follower of Christ means being vulnerable to difficult challenges and risky changes.

Are we complacently *acting* as if we are people of faith, or are we confronting these challenges and responding to God's call in authentic, transforming ways?

• *Reconciliation begins with Christlike love.* In Christ, there are no distinctions. We are free from our earthly labels. We become the body of Christ, and when we love as Christ does, we experience true fellowship with one another.

• *You have the power to bring about real change.* Our daily choices communicate something of who we are to those around us. When we are open to change, God will empower us to make a difference in those around us. But it begins with us!

• *Being the church means being community.* Outside our church walls are people searching for meaning, hope, and love. The church is called to bring *all* people into communion with God, who brings peace, justice, forgiveness, and new life. If we are not reaching out and welcoming in, we are not *being* the church.

Resources

Cain Hope Felder, "The Letter to Philemon," *The New Interpreter's Bible,* vol. 11 (Nashville: Abingdon Press, 2000).

Richard B. Vinson, "Onesimus," *The Mercer Dictionary of the Bible,* ed. Watson E. Mills et al. (Macon GA: Mercer University Press, 1990).

SPEAKING OF CHALLENGE
Philemon 8-16

Introduction

Today's session is the first of four in which we will listen to "voices of the early church." Most of the New Testament reflects the years immediately after the resurrection of Jesus and the gift of the Spirit at the first Christian Pentecost. They were years of energetic missionary activity, as the good news made its way from its predominantly Jewish "center" in Jerusalem to the edges of the largely Gentile world. The book of Acts and the early letters of the Apostle Paul, in particular, tell of the dramatic events and difficult conflicts that led to the inclusion of Gentile Christians in the church. As time passed, the "Gentile question" became less intense, new converts were organized into congregations (usually house churches), and issues of leadership, church government, doctrinal instruction, and ethical conduct became important. The four sessions in this unit invite us to overhear voices from those forming and maturing congregations, voices that help us to live more faithfully as individuals and as congregations.

Today we listen to Paul's heartfelt appeal to Philemon on behalf of Philemon's runaway slave, Onesimus, who had become one of Paul's treasured companions and co-workers. Paul wrote this letter in the early sixties from a prison cell in Rome (though it is possible his confinement was in Ephesus or Caesarea). Philemon was a member of the Colossian church that met in his home (Philem 2). Paul wrote his letters to Philemon and to the Colossians at virtually the same time. Tychicus, one of Paul's partners in ministry, delivered both letters. Making the journey from Rome to Colossae with Tychicus was Onesimus, Philemon's slave. In Colossians 4:8-9, Paul wrote, "I have sent him [Tychicus] to you for this very purpose, so that you may know how we are, and that he may encourage your hearts; he is coming with Onesimus, the faithful and beloved brother, who is one of you. They will tell you about everything here."

The brief letter to Philemon is the most personal correspondence in the New Testament. It is a model of "speaking the truth in love," of addressing challenging issues with gracious and respectful honesty. It also underscores the importance of persuasion rather than coercion and makes the crucial point that freely chosen goodness is far more valuable than imposed goodness.

I. Overview of the Onesimus-Philemon Story

Philemon was a central figure in the church at Colossae, well known for his "love for all the saints and faith toward the Lord Jesus" (v. 4). He was a source of joy and encouragement for Paul and of "refreshment" for the hearts of the Christians in Colossae (v. 7). A slave in Philemon's household, Onesimus, had run away from his duties. Verses 18-19 may indicate that Onesimus had stolen money from Philemon, or simply that Philemon had lost the value of the labor Onesimus would have performed had he not run away. Although the letter does not tell us how or why, Onesimus was in Rome, where he met Paul. Under Paul's influence, Onesimus became a Christian and a valued partner in Paul's ministry.

However, Onesimus could not remain in Rome. He had to go back to Colossae and to Philemon. Paul wrote this letter, entrusted it to Tychicus, and sent both him and Onesimus on their way. Most likely, Paul's simple purpose in writing was to ask Philemon to receive Onesimus with mercy and forgiveness—"no longer as a slave but more than a slave, a beloved brother." Paul appealed to Philemon to welcome Onesimus as he would welcome Paul (v. 17) and promised to "repay" any money Philemon had lost due to Onesimus's defection (vv. 18-19).

John Knox made the fascinating suggestion that Paul had an even bolder purpose in mind: to request that Philemon set Onesimus free to return to Paul's side and to continue his work as Paul's partner. Knox pointed to verse 13—"I wanted to keep him here with me, so that he might be of service to me in your

place during my imprisonment for the gospel"—and to verse 20—
"Yes, brother, let me have this benefit from you in the Lord!
Refresh my heart in Christ!" Knox also referred to the Epistle of
Ignatius, an early second-century letter that mentioned an
Onesimus as the bishop of the church in Ephesus (John Knox,
"The Epistle to Philemon," *Interpreter's Bible Commentary*, vol. 11
[Nashville: Abingdon Press, 1955], 556-60). While most inter-
preters do not share Knox's view that Paul had this bolder
purpose in mind, it remains an intriguing possibility, one that
would show that the early church was already aware of the
tension between Christian equality and the pervasive and largely
unquestioned institution of slavery.

II. Philemon 8-16

Making his request on Onesimus's behalf, Paul wrote, "I am bold
enough in Christ to command you to do your duty, yet I would
rather appeal to you on the basis of love" (vv. 8-9) and "I
preferred to do nothing without your consent, in order that your
good deed might be voluntary and not something forced" (v.14).
While separated by nearly twenty centuries and dealing with
different issues, Paul's preference for Philemon to make a voluntary response resonates with George Truett's famous statement
on religious liberty. Speaking from the east steps of the U.S.
Capitol in 1920, Truett said, "Religion must be forever voluntary
and uncoerced.... God wants free worshipers and no other kind"
(*Baptists and Religious Liberty*, <http://www.bjcpa.org/Pages/
Resources/Pubs/truett.html> 7 Sep, 2004). While it is possible to
compel outward conformity, it is not possible to coerce inward
commitments. Paul sought to persuade, not to command
Philemon, because voluntary goodness—goodness that arises
from the freedom of a heart that has been challenged and
changed by the spirit of God—is more valuable than merely
outward and superficial compliance.

Paul called Onesimus his "child, whose father I have become
during my imprisonment" (v. 10). Paul often referred to his
converts as his "children" (see, for example, Gal 3:19; 1 Tim 1:2,
18; 2 Tim 1:2, 2:1; Titus 1:4), indicating Paul's love and sense of
ongoing responsibility for them. It is not enough to convince

people to become followers of Jesus Christ; they need the continuing guidance and support of the Christian community.

Verse 11 uses a wordplay on the name "Onesimus," which means "useful": "Formerly, he was useless to you, but now he is indeed useful both to you and to me." Verse 12 demonstrates the tenderness Paul felt for Onesimus: to send Onesimus back to Philemon was like sending his own heart. Paul hoped that Philemon would welcome Onesimus back as a "beloved brother" and not as a slave (v. 16)—a brother "in the flesh and in the Lord."

Receiving Onesimus as a brother "in the flesh" would have meant a change in Onesimus's status as a slave and Philemon's status as a slave owner. The essential equality they shared "in the Lord" would have become visible in their relationship to each other. Such a change would have been a rare, even unprecedented realization of the vision Paul described in Galatians 3:28: "There is no longer Jew or Greek, *there is no longer slave or free*, there is no longer male and female; for all of you are one in Christ Jesus." In Colossians 3:11, Paul wrote to Philemon's church, "There is no longer Greek and Jew, circumcised and uncircumcised, barbarian, Scythian, *slave and free*; but Christ is all in all (see also 1 Cor 12:13).

Slavery was practiced in every part of the Roman Empire, and a slave "could be given, let, sold, exchanged, or seized for debt. His person and his life were absolutely in the power of his master" (Marvin R. Vincent, *The Epistles to the Philippians and to Philemon*, International Critical Commentary [Edinburgh: T. & T. Clark, 1979, latest impression], 163). The early Christian movement did not call for the abolition of slavery, but it did encourage humane relationships between slaves and masters. For example, Paul said, "Masters treat your slaves justly and fairly, for you know that you also have a Master in heaven" (Col 4:4). More significantly, the gospel that the church proclaimed eventually served to end the existence of slavery in the vast majority of the world. As Marvin Vincent said, "The principles of the gospel not only curtailed its abuses but destroyed the things itself; for it could not exist without its abuses. To destroy its abuses was to destroy it" (167).

The church's slow progress toward the realization that the gospel of Jesus Christ is incompatible with the practice of slavery can caution us that it is possible to be blind to injustices of which we are a part. The dominant values and expectations of our culture, as well as the long-standing practice of our churches, exercise a powerful hold on our imaginations and make it difficult for us to see some of the places and people in whom God's spirit is now working, without our cooperation, for liberation, justice, and peace.

We do not know how Philemon responded to Paul's appeal and Onesimus's return. For Philemon to set Onesimus free or even to forgive and restore him to his former position would have required Philemon to go against cultural expectations. Were it not for the grace and freedom of the gospel, the challenge Paul placed before him would have been unimaginably hard to meet. Because that challenge was so difficult, it is significant that this letter, while mainly addressed to Philemon, is not exclusively for him. Paul intended for the letter to be read by "Apphia our sister, to Archippus our fellow soldier and to the church in your house" (v. 1). Perhaps Paul knew that Apphia and Archippus were the kind of Christ-followers who would encourage Philemon to meet this challenge. Maybe Paul also counted on the church at Colossae to call upon Philemon to take this risky action. What is more, if Onesimus were welcomed back into Philemon's household, he would also need to be welcomed back into the local congregation. The church would face, as Philemon did, the challenge of forgiveness and reconciliation; and if the church did open its arms to this returned slave, what message would they be sending to their own slaves? By receiving Onesimus, would they be telling their own slaves that the church approved of pushing for freedom? What kind of statement would they be making to their culture? Would even this modest tampering with the issue of slavery bring pressure on their fledgling church? What Paul asked of Philemon and the Colossian church would require a measure of courage rarely possible for an isolated individual. To live in ways that are consistent with the rule and reign of God made known in Jesus Christ, we need the prayers, encouragement, and accountability of the Christian community.

III. Conclusion

We have listened to the challenging voice of Paul as he appealed to Philemon to receive with compassion, and perhaps even to set free, his runaway slave Onesimus. Paul has modeled for us how to appeal to the consciences of our sisters and brothers in Christ, without resorting to coercion and manipulation. He has reminded us of the essential equality of all people. Most significantly, his voice has called us to imagine ways in which we may live with passion and courage in obedience to the often counter-cultural ways of Jesus.

Notes

Notes

2

SPEAKING OF COMMITMENT

2 Timothy 2:1-13

Central Question

How are we to make sense of suffering?

Scripture

2 Timothy 2:1-13 You then, my child, be strong in the grace that is in Christ Jesus; 2 and what you have heard from me through many witnesses entrust to faithful people who will be able to teach others as well. 3 Share in suffering like a good soldier of Christ Jesus. 4 No one serving in the army gets entangled in everyday affairs; the soldier's aim is to please the enlisting officer. 5 And in the case of an athlete, no one is crowned without competing according to the rules. 6 It is the farmer who does the work who ought to have the first share of the crops. 7 Think over what I say, for the Lord will give you understanding in all things. 8 Remember Jesus Christ, raised from the dead, a descendant of David—that is my gospel, 9 for which I suffer hardship, even to the point of being chained like a criminal. But the word of God is not chained. 10 Therefore I endure everything for the sake of the elect, so that they may also obtain the salvation that is in Christ Jesus, with eternal glory. 11 The saying is sure: If we have died with him, we will also live with him; 12 if we endure, we will also reign with him; if we deny him, he will also deny us; 13 if we are faithless, he remains faithful—for he cannot deny himself.

Reflecting

If being a Christian meant being shielded from the difficult things in life, our churches would overflow with committed followers. Whatever the requirements, disciplines, or commitments, they would seem worth it if suffering could be removed from our lives. However, Christians suffer as mightily as anyone else does, which makes the nature of our commitment all the more important. God calls us to be faithful despite suffering.

Timothy, a representative of Paul, had an overwhelming task. Even this energetic missionary found it difficult to remain faithful and disciplined when the negative outweighed the positive. The author wrote to Timothy, empathizing with him because of his sufferings and calling him to remain faithful.

Remembering

Although each letter has its own significance, scholars often group the two New Testament letters to Timothy, along with the letter to Titus, as *Pastoral Epistles* because of their concern for pastoral issues and their similarities in theology and scope. Second Timothy, in particular, stands out from the other Pastorals because of its personal nature.

The three Pastoral Epistles deal with similar circumstances—the organization of the churches, the threat of false teachers, and the importance of exemplary Christian behavior in the world. The term "Pastoral Epistles" was not applied to these letters until the early eighteenth century (Polhill, 649).

Just before our text, Paul gives a testimonial about his unashamed work as a prisoner of the Lord. Obviously concerned about Timothy's willingness to continue his pastoral work, it seems as if the writer was saying to Timothy, "I have been there and done that, and I'm still doing it."

Timothy was responsible for overseeing several churches. However, the work seemed to be falling apart. Immediately following our session's Scripture, Paul names some of the frustrations that had weakened Timothy's devotion (2 Tim 2:14-18). Apparently, people in his congregations were putting their ener-

> Remind them of this, and warn them before God that they are to avoid wrangling over words, which does no good but only ruins those who are listening. Do your best to present yourself to God as one approved by him, a worker who has no need to be ashamed, rightly explaining the word of truth. Avoid profane chatter, for it will lead people into more and more impiety, and their talk will spread like gangrene. Among them are Hymenaeus and Philetus, who have swerved from the truth by claiming that the resurrection has already taken place. They are upsetting the faith of some. (2 Tim 2:14-18)

gies into "wrangling over words" rather than being good listeners (v. 14). Their chatter about worthless things was spreading like a disease throughout the larger community (vv. 16-17). Then, in chapter 3, Paul presents a laundry list of ungodly actions polluting the work of God.

Among these obstacles, early Christians were continuously tempted to follow paths away from God. All three Pastoral Epistles indicate that beliefs and practices of other religions influenced the churches. In addition, social issues continued to divide rather than unite believers.

We are not surprised, then, by Paul's urgency and the passion with which he writes to Timothy. Paul knew how easily adversity kills the spirit. History has shown us repeatedly how easily those without hope for the future lose faith. Even physicians agree that patients with a sense of hope battle illness much better than those who give up. Like an experienced and loving parent, Paul encourages Timothy to "be strong" and true to God's call—even when giving up seems an easier option.

This theme echoes throughout 2 Timothy, as it does with all who find the Christian journey difficult. Interestingly, 1 and 2 Timothy close with the plural form of the Greek word *you*, which suggests that these letters were to be read by all the churches to which Timothy was assigned. These words of challenge and encouragement were not only for Timothy. Paul wrote to help strengthen the resolve of all church members and to confront them with their responsibility to keep the faith. We, too, hear the call to remain faithful, but what is our response?

Studying

Our session's text begins with these words of encouragement to Timothy: be *strong*. The words set the tone for the following verses, but we should not take them as merely a "pat on the back" or a "thumbs-up" from Timothy's mentor, who makes a serious charge to Timothy that he remain fully committed to his duty, even in suffering. This encouragement is based not on a glib belief that "all's well that ends well," but rather on the hopeful belief that even the worst life offers cannot ultimately overcome God's grace. Paul works with the fundamental belief that this world is God's; therefore, God always has the last word. That affirmation is the stronghold of hope. It is little wonder that the passage ends with a short poem or hymn to remind Timothy of why he must be strong and endure.

It is not unusual that Paul refers to Timothy as "my child" (v. 1). Timothy's mother and grandmother had raised him in the Christian faith (2 Tim 1:5), but Paul adopted him as a beloved friend and co-worker. Paul became Timothy's mentor and teacher throughout his ministry.

After Paul encourages Timothy to find strength "in the grace that is in Christ Jesus," he reminds his co-worker of the impor-

> Paul held Timothy in high regard. In at least one instance, Paul intimates that Timothy should be ranked among the apostles (see 1 Thess 2:6) (Ciholas, 920).

tant task at hand—to continue passing on the traditions of the faith just as others had done for him. Within the traditions passed on to Timothy is the basis of hope that Timothy must rely upon in his own ministry. Stories from the past reminded Timothy of God's work with Moses and Sarah, God's grace with Adam and Eve, and God's steadfast love for Israel and the Gentiles.

Like any good teacher or communicator, Paul uses metaphors to help readers better understand his message. He describes the farmer who works tirelessly to reap a good crop, the athlete who must endure the difficulties of training in order to be crowned champion, and the soldier who is never distracted from his duty.

He hopes his readers will ponder these examples, looking to the Lord for better understanding (v. 7).

Readers would have been familiar with each example Paul gave. Many of them were farmers, so they knew the dedication required to produce a successful harvest. The soldier metaphor provides a similar example, for the soldier must be single-minded in his duty, never straying from the orders of his officer. As James Dunn notes, "Since many successful military veterans retired to farm land granted them by the state, the two images (soldier and farmer) went naturally together" (842).

The recipients of this letter were also familiar with the great athletic contests held in surrounding Greek cities. They knew of the incredible discipline it took to compete and win. Interestingly, the farmer, athlete, and soldier are still relevant images today. They are all unique, but they share common thoughts: *Stay committed. Stay focused. Endure.*

In verses 8-10, Paul encourages Timothy by citing why they must endure: "Remember Jesus Christ, raised from the dead" (v. 8a). The gospel is good news. Because Jesus was raised from the dead, we have new life in Christ and eternal life to come. Paul charges Timothy and the churches Timothy served to remember Christ in every situation. Christ gives strength and grace when suffering seems unbearable. Even when Paul was persecuted to the point of imprisonment, he recognized God working through his weakness (v. 9). God's word echoes through the prison walls and into the world.

In verse 10, Paul mentions the "elect" as those who may *also* experience salvation in Christ Jesus. Paul understood the elect as those now able to obtain the salvation God promised to the people of Israel. The good news is for all people, and Paul was willing to suffer hardship so that Jews and Gentiles would have the opportunity for salvation.

Paul sums up his charge to Timothy with four carefully crafted phrases that read like a hymn. Each line provides a paradox of ideas. If we die with Christ, we will also live with Christ. If we endure, we will also reign. In the third line, there is no upswing. If we deny him, he will deny us. Lastly, the fourth line states that God will always remain faithful. In other words, it is God's nature to be committed to the people God created. God intends salvation for all people. It is God's desire for people to know of love, hope, and joy.

Understanding

Like a masterful artist, the author of this Scripture blends images of common people with deep commitments, along with his own experience of hardship, to create a portrait of what it means to share in suffering for the sake of Christ. In addition, as a true piece of art, the metaphors, images, and poetry in this text communicate far beyond the cultural setting of Timothy's time. The theme of suffering and the call to committed duty speak to us today.

Why do people suffer? This troubling question has caused many good and prospective followers to stumble. We wonder how God can allow our personal suffering and the suffering of our world. In *The Wounded Healer*, theologian and minister Henri Nouwen explains how through our own struggles and pain, as wounded people ourselves, we have a genuine connection with others. At the same time, empowered with the gifts of God and the gospel, we have a message of healing and hope that knows no boundaries. Because of our suffering, we are wounded healers with much to offer and receive from others as we minister.

? When has your suffering allowed you to minister to someone else?

As Christians, our common faith allows us to share our joys and pains with one another. We gain hope when we can walk through the valleys of life together. Not only can we be present with one another in difficult times, but we can also be healed of our fear, hopelessness, anxiety, and even of our faithlessness through the gospel. Even when we are not able to have hope, or to be faithful on our own, we remember and know that God is faithful and strong for us.

What About Me?

• *The very nature of God is to love and care for us.* No matter how angry, troubled, frightened, or hopeless we are, God remains faithful, providing strength for us to endure.

• *Decide to be disciplined.* There is no middle ground. Decide today to be disciplined in your walk with God.

• *You are not alone in your suffering.* While it may seem as if no one else can understand our suffering, Christ suffered as we do. Christ knows our pain, and his presence sustains us.

Resources

Paul Ciholas, "Timothy," *The Mercer Dictionary of the Bible,* ed. Watson E. Mills et al. (Macon GA: Mercer University Press, 1990).

James D. G. Dunn, "First and Second Timothy and Titus," *The New Interpreter's Bible,* vol. 11 (Nashville: Abingdon Press, 2000).

John B. Polhill, "Pastoral Epistles," *The Mercer Dictionary of the Bible,* ed. Watson E. Mills et al. (Macon GA: Mercer University Press, 1990).

SPEAKING OF COMMITMENT
2 Timothy 2:1-13

Introduction

The sessions for the next two weeks come from two of the three "Pastoral Epistles" (1 and 2 Timothy and Titus). Written to church leaders associated with the Apostle Paul, these writings offer counsel on how to nurture and guide Christian communities. Thomas Oden wrote, "'Pastoral letters' do not mean 'to be ignored by the laity.' They address questions crucial to the health of the laity—the life of prayer, the meaning of public worship, care for the needy and poor, and sound teaching as the basis for holy living" (*First and Second Timothy and Titus*, Interpretation: A Bible Commentary for Teaching and Preaching [Louisville: John Knox Press, 1989], 1).

Traditionally, the Pastoral Epistles have been attributed to the Apostle Paul, and there is solid evidence that they are his writings; however, the letters also contain some vocabulary and doctrinal concerns that do not appear in those New Testament letters which no one doubts that Paul wrote. In this week's commentary, I work with the assumption that, despite the difficulties, Paul wrote the bulk of the material in the Pastoral Epistles, but the important meaning of these texts does not, finally, depend upon the identity of the seasoned church leader who offered his experience and wisdom to a succeeding generation. (Both Thomas Oden, *First and Second Timothy and Titus*, and Glenn Hinson, "1-2 Timothy and Titus," *The Broadman Bible Commentary*, vol. 11 [Nashville: Broadman Press, 1967] sift the issues carefully and lean toward Paul's authorship of the Pastorals.)

Paul likely wrote 2 Timothy in the mid-sixties, while imprisoned in Rome. Timothy was Paul's younger friend and protégé. They met during Paul's initial missionary journey to Lystra (see Acts 13:1–14:28). Like the other Pastoral Epistles, 2 Timothy focuses on the faithful endurance and healthy maturity churches and their leaders need to maintain a strong and vibrant Christian witness in the face of tension and opposition.

I. "Be Strong in Grace," 2:1-7.

"You *then*, my child, be strong in the grace that is in Christ Jesus" (v. 1). *Then* points us back to the encouragement Paul gave Timothy in the first chapter of this letter. Timothy faced difficult issues, but Paul assured him that he could rise to the challenge: Timothy had a strong legacy of faith, extending back to his mother and grandmother (1:5), and he had a "gift of God," confirmed by "the laying on of Paul's hands" (1:6). What's more, Paul said, "God did not give us a spirit of cowardice, but rather a spirit of power and love and of self discipline" (1:7). "Be strong," Paul urged Timothy, "in *the grace* that is in Christ Jesus." Strength comes from our cooperation with grace; it grows out of our faith, our openness to God's gifts, and our responsiveness to the presence of God.

What does "being strong in grace" look like? Our text offers three metaphors of strength: a "good soldier of Jesus Christ" (vv. 3-4), an "athlete" (v. 5), and a "farmer" (v. 7). Oden wrote, "From the soldier one learns obedience; from the athlete disciplined preparation; from the farmer, steady, patient persistence" (163).

We need to use the "good soldier" metaphor wisely. In language that echoes our text, Ephesians 6:10-13 says, "Be strong in the Lord and in the strength of his power. Put on the whole armor of God, so that you may be able to stand against the wiles of the devil. For our struggle is not against blood and flesh, but against the rulers, against the authorities, against the cosmic powers of this present darkness, against the spiritual forces of evil in the heavenly places. Therefore, take up the whole armor of God." Christians are "soldiers" whose "fight" is against evil, not against other human beings.

Paul underscores that a "good soldier" avoids, as much as possible, entanglement in "everyday affairs" and has the single aim of "pleasing the enlisting officer" (v. 4). A soldier also knows that he might be called upon to suffer (v. 3) in pursuit of obedience. There are times, this metaphor admits, when commitment to the way of Jesus Christ brings us into uncomfortable tension with the dominant ways of our culture.

Being strong in grace is as the discipline of an "athlete" who "competes according to the rules" (v. 5). What "rules" did Paul have in mind—the "rules of the game" ("run in your own lane" or "three strikes and you're out") or the "rules of preparation" (good nutrition, working with a knowledgeable coach, and engaging in thorough training)? Perhaps Paul had both in view. The most decorated Olympian of all time, Michael Phelps' well-deserved victories depended upon attention to both kinds of rules—the rules of the game and the rules of preparation. His commitment and endurance prepared him for the pinnacle of competition held just once every four years, highlighting the difficulty of his remarkable achievements. These unparalleled successes are even more astonishing considering he achieved them over four consecutive Olympic games. Still, these achievements, would not have been possible if not for Phelps's honorable conduct and respect for the competition and for the rules themselves.

Lewis Donelson makes the intriguing suggestion that the "rules" are spelled out in the hymn in 2:11-13: "The true rules of the cosmos, the rules of the Christian life, are found in the story of Jesus Christ" (*Colossians, Ephesians, First and Second Timothy and Titus*, Westminster Bible Companion [Louisville: Westminster John Knox Press, 1996], 157). The "Christian athlete" lives by the contradictory "rules" made true by the cross and empty tomb. The self-denial that is a necessary part of athletic discipline points to the words of Jesus: "If any want to become my followers, let them deny themselves and take up their cross and follow me.... Those who lose their life for my sake, and for the sake of the gospel, will save it" (Mk 8:34-35). The central "rule" is this: "If we have died with him, we will also live with him" (2 Tim 2:11).

Being strong in grace is also like the steady work of a "farmer" (v. 6). While Paul mentions the reward due a hard-working farmer—who "ought to have the first share of the crops"—he includes the metaphor of farmer to emphasize that Christian faithfulness is like the ongoing attentiveness and labor of one who works the land. Of his Kentucky farm, Wendell Berry once wrote, "I have made this place my life. I am its dependent; it is my dependent.... Our place shows clearly its dependence, not so much on the conscious large acts such as a man might do out of duty, but on the hundreds of trivial acts that a man who loves it does every day, without pre-meditation, in the course of doing other things" (Wendell Berry, *A Continuous Harmony, Essays Cultural and Agricultural* [New York: Harcourt Brace Jovanovich, 1972], 43-44). Fidelity to Jesus Christ and his church finds expression not just in the necessary things we might do out of duty, but in the myriad smaller things we do out of love. We depend upon the church to support us, teach us, "feed" us, and encourage us, but we also recognize that the vitality and productivity of the church depend, in part, upon our own attentiveness to its health.

Soldier, athlete, and farmer—these metaphors of "being strong in grace" call us to tenacious and disciplined commitment. Paul wanted Timothy to exercise gracious strength in pursuit of a par-ticular purpose: "What you have heard from me through many witnesses entrust to faithful people who will be able to teach others as well" (v. 2). The Christian story lives, from generation to generation, in the thoughtful and passionate witness of Christians. To bear such witness, sometimes under external pressure from the culture and sometimes under internal pressure from our own struggles, we need the strength this text describes, strength that comes from God's grace and our committed response to it.

II. "Remember Jesus Christ...Who Remains Faithful," 2:8-13.

This section begins with a brief confession of faith, a confession Paul calls "my gospel": "Remember Jesus Christ, raised from the dead, a descendant of David" (v. 8). This confession is likely a fragment of a reading commonly used in worship and in the instruction of new converts. It declares both the divinity (raised from the dead) and the humanity (descended from David) of Jesus. Thomas Oden wrote, "Only if Christ is human can he feel our infirmities. Only if Christ is God does his death have atoning value for all humanity." It is significant that an affirmation of Jesus' resurrection comes first, and then acknowledgement of his human origins. Christian faith is centered on Easter and, from experience of resurrection, reaches "back" to Christmas and the incarnation and "forward" to Pentecost and the gift of the Spirit.

Paul viewed his imprisonment as being for the sake of the gospel; he was in chains, but he said, "The word of God is not chained" (v. 9). The human servants of God's word can be constrained, even silenced, but the word remains free and power-ful. John Bunyan's *Pilgrim's Progress*, Dietrich Bonhoeffer's *Letters and Papers from Prison*, Father Alfred Delp's *Prison Meditations*, and Martin Luther King Jr.'s "Letter from Birmingham Jail" make Paul's point: the gospel can make its way past the bars of a prison cell. Jailed, Paul said to the Philippians, "What has happened to me has actually helped to spread the gospel" (1:12).

Paul thought of his imprisonment as an experience to be "endured for the sake of the elect" (v. 10a). "The elect" simply means "chosen" and refers to all who had, or would, become followers of Christ. Paul knew that his struggle bore witness to the power of the gospel, a witness that called upon others to "obtain the salvation that is in Christ Jesus, with eternal glory" (v. 10b).

In verses 11-13, Paul draws from a hymn from early church worship, probably used in connection with the celebration of baptism. Verse 11, about dying and living with Jesus, is very simi-lar to Romans 6:8, which is part of an extended reflection on baptism as the enactment of union with the death and resurrec-tion of Christ. The experience of baptism is the beginning, not the culmination, of a life of discipleship that calls for faithful endurance: "If we endure, we will also reign with him" (v. 12a). The opposite of such endurance is denial of Jesus, which the hymn sternly cautions against (v. 12b). "He also will deny us" is an echo of Jesus' stark words in Matthew 10:33: "Whoever denies me before others, I also will deny before my Father in heaven."

In saving tension with this warning against denial, the hymn's last phrase makes a bold assertion about God's faithfulness, a faithfulness that is stronger than human faithlessness (v. 13a). Although we are capable of denial, God "cannot deny himself" (v. 13b). God cannot be untrue to the divine nature, which is love, and God never stops doing what God did in the life, death, and resurrection of Jesus: freely offering grace to everyone—to those who welcomed it and to those who rejected it. By use of this hymn, Paul seems to have been saying, "While God will, in the end and with deep sorrow, respect an individual's rejection of Jesus Christ, until that rejection is final, God will not stop trying to reverse it." God seeks to turn every "no" into a "yes"; God always, with relentless tenderness, pours out the divine life to persuade all people of God's great love.

Conclusion

Through this text, we have heard the voice of one of the early church's seasoned leaders, who challenged Timothy to be strong in his commitment to Jesus Christ. Paul's words ring with power and authenticity, because they were forged from his own costly com-mitment to the gospel. Ultimately, such commitment—Paul's or Timothy's or ours—is rooted in the prior commitment of God to us.

Notes

Notes

SPEAKING OF
PUBLIC BEHAVIOR

Titus 3:1-11

Central Question

How does being a Christian affect our actions?

Scripture

Titus 3:1-11 Remind them to be subject to rulers and authorities, to be obedient, to be ready for every good work, 2 to speak evil of no one, to avoid quarreling, to be gentle, and to show every courtesy to everyone. 3 For we ourselves were once foolish, disobedient, led astray, slaves to various passions and pleasures, passing our days in malice and envy, despicable, hating one another. 4 But when the goodness and loving kindness of God our Savior appeared, 5 he saved us, not because of any works of righteousness that we had done, but according to his mercy, through the water of rebirth and renewal by the Holy Spirit. 6 This Spirit he poured out on us richly through Jesus Christ our Savior, 7 so that, having been justified by his grace, we might become heirs according to the hope of eternal life. 8 The saying is sure. I desire that you insist on these things, so that those who have come to believe in God may be careful to devote themselves to good works; these things are excellent and profitable to everyone. 9 But avoid stupid controversies, genealogies, dissensions, and quarrels about the law, for they are unprofitable and worthless. 10 After a first and second admonition, have nothing more to do with anyone who causes divisions, 11 since you know that such a person is perverted and sinful, being self-condemned.

Reflecting

Gracias! is the journal of theologian and pastor Henri Nouwen as he traveled through Bolivia and Peru. During the journey, Nouwen recalled his own spiritual journey of discerning God's call. He explains that his original desires were to be useful, to do something significant, or to be a part of an impressive project. However, as he matured in faith and experience, Nouwen realized that the simple ministry of *presence* in people's lives can be more powerful than an organized program or large mission. After pondering his time spent in meetings, conferences, and workshops, he wrote, "I wonder more and more if the first thing shouldn't be to know people by name, to eat and to drink with them, to listen to their stories and tell your own, and to let them know with words, handshakes, and hugs that you do not simply like them, but truly love them" (147-48).

Sometimes we think it takes bold programs to bring people to church. Nouwen believes we encounter God and experience God's love in daily relationships. In other words, our mission endeavors are more about acting out what we say we believe. Our public behavior teaches others about our faith before we utter any words. Our behavior can open the door for ministry in greater ways than we often imagine.

Today's text is addressed to a church divided. The ministry of the church in Crete was weakening. Paul reminds church members simply to do good things for their brothers and sisters so that people will be receptive to the message of the gospel. Many years ago, Francis of Assisi summarized this idea well: "Preach the gospel always; if necessary, use words."

Remembering

In our last session, we reviewed the ongoing hardship and persecution of the early church. The original readers of 2 Timothy struggled simply to endure. Yet Paul urged them to continue working at their discipline. The theme of persecution continues in Titus, though the context is a bit different.

The letter to Titus indicates that Paul and Titus had traveled to Crete to carry out the administration of the church. Like the other Pastoral Epistles, it is difficult to determine the date of writing. The book of Acts mentions a visit to Greece (Acts 20:3), which may have included some time in Crete. In 2 Timothy, the author places Titus in Dalmatia (2 Tim 4:10).

The setting presumes that Paul left Titus in Crete to continue the organization and administration of the church there. Paul needed to make Titus aware of the terrible reputation the Cretans had earned. He also offered advice on how to avoid "stupid controversies" and focus on the good that could be done (Titus 3:8-9).

The beginning of the letter includes the usual Pauline salutation and greeting, followed immediately by a description of the work he had for Titus. Titus's main responsibility would be to appoint leaders within the church, so Paul provided a checklist by which to judge each candidate. Ironically, after urging Titus to find "blameless" leaders, Paul describes the Cretan community as "corrupt and unbelieving" (Titus 1:15-16). Apparently, not all were unfit, and even for those who were, there was time for change.

In the verses just before our text, Paul focuses on ways to improve the attitudes and actions of the people, giving Titus advice about moving the Cretans toward an understanding of God's grace and a zeal for good deeds (Titus 2). Whereas in chapter 2 Paul focuses on relationships within the Christian community, in chapter 3 he explains how Christians' public behaviors either build or diminish their relationships to the larger community.

Studying

The letter to Titus is the third of the Pastoral Epistles. Titus was Paul's fellow missionary and companion. Second Corinthians, Galatians, and 2 Timothy all mention him. Like Timothy, Titus was Greek by background. In fact, in Galatians, we read that Titus accompanied Paul to Jerusalem for a meeting with the Jerusalem leaders. At this meeting, Titus became the focus of

debate. Because he was Greek, the Judaizers demanded that he be circumcised according to the law. Instead, the apostles present affirmed Paul's work among the Gentiles; therefore, Titus remained uncircumcised. After many years, Paul's belief that the gospel was a message for both Jew and Gentile was acknowledged.

Titus may have been one of Paul's early converts. The salutation in the letter to Titus supports this claim, as Paul refers to him as "my loyal child in the faith we share" (v. 4). Moreover, Paul and Titus formed a trusting relationship and shared a common mission.

Paul even trusted Titus to work through some of the problems that had developed in the church at Corinth. Apparently, Titus was skilled at restoring relationships (particularly between Paul and the churches), and after much anticipation, Titus returned to Paul with good news. Titus reported that he was successful in renewing the Corinthians' zeal for Paul and his ministry.

Because of Titus's successful efforts, Paul urged him to return to Corinth to organize and implement a monetary offering for the church in Jerusalem.

Much like 1 Timothy, the letter to Titus focuses on the ongoing administration and inner workings of the church—appointing leaders and elders, responding to false teachers, and creating working relationships within the family. Paul mentions the terrible reputation of the Cretans, using several long lists of negative traits to describe their corrupt behavior. Apparently, this community was known for its rebellious nature, laziness, deceptive teaching, disobedience, and other faults (see Titus 1:10-16). In fact, the ancient colloquialism "to Cretanize" means to lie (*New Oxford Annotated Bible* [NOAB], 312). We can only imagine the persecution the early church in Crete must have faced in such a harsh environment. The final chapter points to the work of the church in this adverse society. The author gives advice on how the church is to relate to one another, but more importantly how the church is to relate to outsiders.

In this session's Scripture, Paul provides a list of *dos* and *don'ts* for public behavior. He also reminds the Cretans why they are called to do good works. In Pauline fashion, he claims that the gospel of Jesus Christ is our sole reason for experiencing hope and life; as a result, we are to live as people of hope and love. Unfortunately, the people of this church seemed to have little faith. The letter includes basic instructions on how to get along and act appropriately, along with a reminder that what others see in you determines how they interpret the gospel.

The church's relationship with rulers and authorities requires obedience and a readiness to do good things, says Paul (v. 1). With all people, they are to be gentle, peaceful, and kind (v. 2). This lifestyle is not to be superficial, nor is it intended to be merely politically correct. Paul reminds them that formerly they were "despicable" and "foolish" wanderers who lived in hatred and envy, with no hope and no direction in life (v. 3). Now, through grace and mercy, God has transformed them and given them a new life—one birthed in goodness and love. No longer are they living to die, but because of Christ's death, they now have abundant and eternal life.

In 3:5, the descriptive illustration of water washing away sins and giving sustenance to begin a new life points to the act of baptism (*NOAB*, 313). The pouring out of the Holy Spirit provides a picture of a rich outer covering of God's grace and hope that every believer wears. Paul then calls Titus and the Cretans to "devote themselves to good works" (v. 8). It is not enough merely to speak of good things or talk about our faith. God calls believers to *live* out our faith through actions.

Titus 3:9 includes another list of actions for the Cretans to avoid. Paul warns Titus of things that have caused problems in the past, encouraging him to be proactive in preventing these things from causing more division. Most of the controversies involved arguments about the law. Again, it seems that the religious establishment was relentless in its efforts to alienate and divide. Because of their selfish motives and unwillingness to change, Paul gives church members advice on excluding these false teachers from the fellowship of faith. Still, they are to give more than one opportunity for the "dividers" to change their ways before having nothing more to do with them. Notice the emphasis on grace before condemnation!

People were even debating genealogies. Needlessly, teachers of the law were speculating whose line of family history showed more faith.

Understanding

An age-old question surfaces in this text: Is faith or works more important? At times, Paul's theology seems to give more weight to one or the other, and in this text, the focus is on works. He advises Christians to do good *works* both inside and outside the church. So is Paul assuming that *works* is the way to save the community? He definitely wanted the Cretans to *insist* on good works, but does that mean to push faith aside?

The answer is actually quite clear. Paul preached salvation by grace. We cannot earn salvation. We are all on equal footing under the mercy of Christ. However, from our salvation flows good action. Through the Holy Spirit, we are *moved* to be like Christ and to do good. Faith and works go hand in hand. We cannot become righteous by what we do, but we cannot be righteous without bearing fruit. That basic understanding should have been evident from the beginning of their Christian journey, yet Titus had to remind his community that salvation is a process.

Living out our faith is a clear sign of a change within us. It is evidence of the inner transformation. The world looks to us for evidence of the truth of the gospel. If we do not show evidence of that transformation, how can anyone believe? In us, the world experiences God on earth as we act as the visible hands, feet, heart, and body of Christ. It is in our daily encounters that we can reveal God's goodness. Sometimes we expect God to do something big that will attract people. Yet, even through our small deeds, God works in the world. Our actions matter because they reveal to whom we belong.

What About Me?

• *Point to God in everything.* People need God's presence in their lives. As Christians, we have the responsibility to point out the work of God when we recognize it.

• *Faith does work!* A healthy faith is one that moves us to act! Reaching out to others involves *living out* our faith in tangible and meaningful ways. Sometimes a simple act of kindness or mercy will provide an opportunity to share faith.

• *Gracefully avoid pettiness.* Most often, divisions in our congregations or families begin with small controversies over silly things. We must wrestle through these problems, offering grace along the way. Yet we should use discernment and know when to avoid the ones that continually make life difficult.

• *Be people of presence.* Programs are useful, but people bear witness to Christ. Be present in the lives of your brothers and sisters. Building relationships is the key to building the church.

Resources

James D. G. Dunn, "First and Second Timothy and Titus," *The New Interpreter's Bible,* vol. 11 (Nashville: Abingdon Press, 2000).

Henri J. M. Nouwen, *Gracias!: A Latin American Journal* (Maryknoll NY: Orbis Books, 1983).

The New Oxford Annotated Bible (New York: Oxford University Press, 1991).

SPEAKING OF PUBLIC BEHAVIOR
Titus 3:1-11

Introduction

Our public behavior reflects our private being. How we behave on the outside grows out of who we are inside. Who we are on the inside is grounded in the grace of God. When we receive God's grace our assignment is to pass it on. This is the great joy in life: to learn to be God's partner in grace and giving.

In this Titus passage, Paul encourages believers to behave as believers, not as pagans. He invites us to express our faith not only in words or feelings, but also through our behavior. We must act as people who have received the spirit of God through the grace of God, for how we allow God to shape us inside shows up in how we treat people and how we behave in public.

During the funeral of President Reagan, in the summer of 2004, I was struck by how often the media raised the question, "What has happened to the civility we used to have in this country? Why so many ugly slurs and irresponsible attacks of each other in politics, schools, churches, the media, and the Internet?" Mr. Reagan was described as a "graceful" man who could turn an enemy into a friend. He was able to "disagree agreeably." One did not have to share Reagan's politics to appreciate his gracious demeanor. His friendship with Tip O'Neill, a Democrat, illustrates his effort to behave with civility as a gracious human being.

I was moved when former President George H. Bush said about his boss, "I have learned more from this man than from any other person in public life." His voice broke, his eyes became teary, and then he spoke of "kindness." What has to kindness, and how can we recover it? Our world sorely needs this week's Scripture lesson.

Titus's readers were victims of persecution and ridicule, powerless and disenfranchised. Such a lowly state made it easy for them to be critical—both about "rulers and authorities" and about people in general. Paul asked Titus to confront this destructive tendency and lead church members to base their behavior on their internal relationship with God—nothing less.

I. How Do We Relate to People—Those Over Us as Well as Our Peers? 3:1-3.

Every organization, even democratic church governments, has "authorities," people who have more power than ordinary people. How do we relate to such people? To put it negatively: Don't be rebellious. To put it positively: Be kind. It's a question of how we will spend our energy. Will we criticize and strike back, or will we "be big hearted and courteous"? (Eugene Peterson, *The Message* [Colorado Springs: NavPress, 2002] v. 2).

The end work of God's grace is that we become gracious ourselves. In our attitudes and treatment of others, God calls us to pass on to others the grace we have received from God. We do this not because they earn or deserve it, but because we are called to treat others as God has treated us.

The history of our world and the experience of our churches illustrate that (1) criticism tends to breed stronger criticism, (2) violence spawns more bitter violence, (3) rebellion incites additional hateful rebellion, and (4) cruelty produces still more evil cruelty.

This Scripture gives us good leadership: "Speak evil of no one, avoid quarreling, be gentle, show courtesy to everyone" (v. 2). Another of Paul's letters says it well: "Be kind to one another" (Eph 4:32).

Grace produces grace; kindness begets kindness; fairness encourages fairness; peacemaking creates peace.

Before becoming believers, before being saved from our lost, broken selves, we ourselves had bad attitudes and treated other people badly. We were once "foolish, rebellious, led astray...passing our days in malice and envy" (vv. 3-4). When we turned to

God and away from self-centeredness, God's spirit washed us clean of this rancor and made us new. God gave us a new attitude and called us into a new way of kindly behavior.

Before Christ became our Lord, Paul says, "We hated everyone; everyone hated us" (v. 3). Now, in Christ, we have a new spirit and a new approach to others. We refuse to return cruelty for cruelty. Instead, we follow the model of our Lord.

II. Where Do We Get the Power to Behave Graciously? 3:4-9.

We humans can't seem to just decide to be gracious, fair, and kind, and then do so. Paul himself admitted, "I can will what is right, but I cannot do it. I do not do the good I want, but the evil I do not want is what I do" (Rom 7:18-19).

You and I recognize this problem as clearly as Paul did. I am prone to be harsh and ugly when I disagree—to attack or gossip rather than discuss. Paul cried out, "O wretched man that I am, who will deliver me from this body of death?" (Rom 7:24). We cannot achieve godly attitudes and behaviors in our own strength. However, we *can* decide to let God continue to redeem us. We cannot be saved by our good deeds or produce good behaviors by a mighty act of human will, but we can be saved by the power of God to do for us what we cannot do for ourselves. My acceptance of God's lordship causes me to want to treat other people as God treats me.

Paul echoes in Titus 3:4-7 what he said to the Ephesian believers: "We are saved by *grace* through faith. And this is not your own doing, it is a *gift* of God.... For we are God's workmanship, created in Christ Jesus for good works" (Eph 2:8-10). In Titus 3:4-7, Paul uses six words or phrases to describe what happens when we accept Christ: "saved," "washed," "renewed in the Holy Spirit," "justified by God's grace," "heirs in God's hope," and "eternal life." Let's ponder these words as we continue to explore godly behavior.

It seems that the key to behaving in godly ways is based on three things:
(1) My life does not belong to me; it is a gift of God. If I claim ownership of my life, I sin in the same way Adam and Eve did in

the garden (Gen 3:1-7) and the builders of the tower of Babel did later in a fiasco of human pride (Gen 11:1-9). Paul said, "Your life is not your own, you are bought with a price" (1 Cor 6:19-20). I must accept the truth that I did not create myself and I cannot redeem myself. My life is not mine to do with as I please. I am here *on assignment.*

(2) Salvation has at least as much to do with life in the present as afterlife in heaven. As important as one's eternal destiny is, "eternal life" in the Bible does not refer exclusively to heaven. The emphasis is on the quality of life, not the quantity. Eternal life (being saved) means first to be renewed by the power of the spirit of God so that my brokenness is made whole, that my lostness and wandering is grounded in God, who gives me new life *now.* Such life will be known fully in heaven.

(3) Grace from God is to be *passed on* to other people. Receiving the gift of grace makes me into a gracious person and a giver of grace myself—even to people who do not deserve grace, as I do not.

"Gift" and "grace" are interesting words. Consider the development of the word grace:
• GRACE in Greek is *charis* (KAR–iss), meaning free, unmerited favor of God.
• GIFT has the same root (*char*), and the word is *charisma* (KAR-iss-ma). It means a free gift that one does not earn or deserve. Paul says we all have *charisma* (1 Cor 12:7, 11).
• JOY is *chara* (kar-AH), meaning a well-being not based on events or environment. Joy is the outcome of accepting the grace and gifts of God, then using those gifts in service and ministry for God.
• THANKSGIVING is also from the root *char—eucharisto* (u-kar-ISS-toe). When we receive God's grace and gifts and then discover the joy of putting them into action, we are naturally giving thanks.

To *show* gratitude is more than feeling. It's thanks-GIVING, not thanks-FEELING. We use this word at the Lord's Supper. There we symbolize God's gift by breaking the bread and pouring the cup. We also symbolize giving our lives to God—their rightful owner—by eating the bread, drinking the cup, and sharing the grace God has given us with others. This idea is Paul's point with Titus.

We demonstrate thanksgiving to God by expressing grace to others as Jesus does to us. We are empowered to live as Christians when grace has made its redeeming cycle from Grace to Gift to Joy to Thanksgiving. Visualize this circle as a clock: GRACE at 12:00, GIFT at 3:00, JOY at 6:00, ThanksGIVING at 9:00, and GRACE again at 12:00. The circle continues as we discover the joy and participation of being grace-givers. When our maturity arrives at 9 o'clock and we GIVE thanks, we do it by moving on to 12 o'clock and becoming partners with God in giving grace freely to others. The circle of grace continues and becomes more potent, pervasive, and joyous.

Verse 3 says, "Once we were takers." We saw life as an entitlement to take whatever we had the power to take and "pass our days in malice and envy." Verse 4 says that we can partner with God's grace and become givers, not takers, treating others as God treats us. But what if someone intentionally disrupts and divides?

III. How Do We Deal with a Disrupter? 3:10-11.

Paul's teaching is clear. First, continue practicing the cycle of grace yourself. Choose to have a good attitude. Treat others with dignity and respect. Do good things for others. You can't always choose your environment, but you can choose your attitude.

Second, "avoid stupid controversies, genealogies, dissensions, and quarrels over the law. For these are unprofitable and futile" (vv. 9-10). "It takes two to have a mud fight," my dad used to tell me. I hear Paul saying:
• Do not counterattack. Do not return rancor for rancor, thus escalating the conflict.
• Talk *with* the person, not *about* the person. In other words, communicate with a disrupter—admonish the behavior while respecting the person. Talk openly about the problems being created. Seek grace together.
• If neither of the above does not calm the disruption and include the divider into the circle of grace, simply withdraw. Let him "cut himself off" (*The Message*, v. 11). The disruptive person is "self-condemned."

Conclusion

Relationships and behavior are neither simple nor automatic. They will not take care of themselves, nor can they be taken for granted. Like a garden, marriage, business, or friendship, they must be planted, then consistently tended and nurtured. Speaking evil of or quarreling with others is like planting weeds in your own garden. Someone said, "Carrying hostility toward someone in your heart is like drinking poison and expecting the other person to die."

God has given us grace and forgiveness we don't deserve. Will we do less for others?

Notes

Notes

SPEAKING OF PERSECUTION

Jude 17-23

Central Question

How do we deal with divisions in our communities of faith?

Scripture

Jude 17-23 But you, beloved, must remember the predictions of the apostles of our Lord Jesus Christ; 18 for they said to you, "In the last time there will be scoffers, indulging their own ungodly lusts." 19 It is these worldly people, devoid of the Spirit, who are causing divisions. 20 But you, beloved, build yourselves up on your most holy faith; pray in the Holy Spirit; 21 keep yourselves in the love of God; look forward to the mercy of our Lord Jesus Christ that leads to eternal life. 22 And have mercy on some who are wavering; 23 save others by snatching them out of the fire; and have mercy on still others with fear, hating even the tunic defiled by their bodies.

Reflecting

When my husband interviewed for his first pastorate, he wondered what he was getting into. The first three churches he dialogued with informed him of major church conflicts within the past five years. Each church had split, and all were still healing from the pain caused by the conflict. Sad to say, many congregations have their own stories of conflict and divisiveness. However, conflict is not a new problem for the church.

If you think the Christian community has only recently faced major problems, then look at the letter of Jude. The Christian community was barely surviving under the influence of the "intruders" and "perverters" of the faith. Church members were struggling to keep other problems from dividing them even more.

While division and conflict are still common in churches today, it would be impossible for us to fully understand the persecution the early Christian community faced. For them, the situation could at times be a matter of life or death. In less violent times, "scoffers" made life difficult. These kinds of folks are still around today, even within the church itself. How are we to deal with scoffers in our lives and in our churches? What is the Christian response to divisions within the faith community?

Roman influence reached wide and far. During the days of Jude's letter, persecution was common. Rome tolerated Christianity for a time but in the end saw it as a divergent sect. In many communities, Christians were the butt of jokes and false accusations, as well as torture and death.

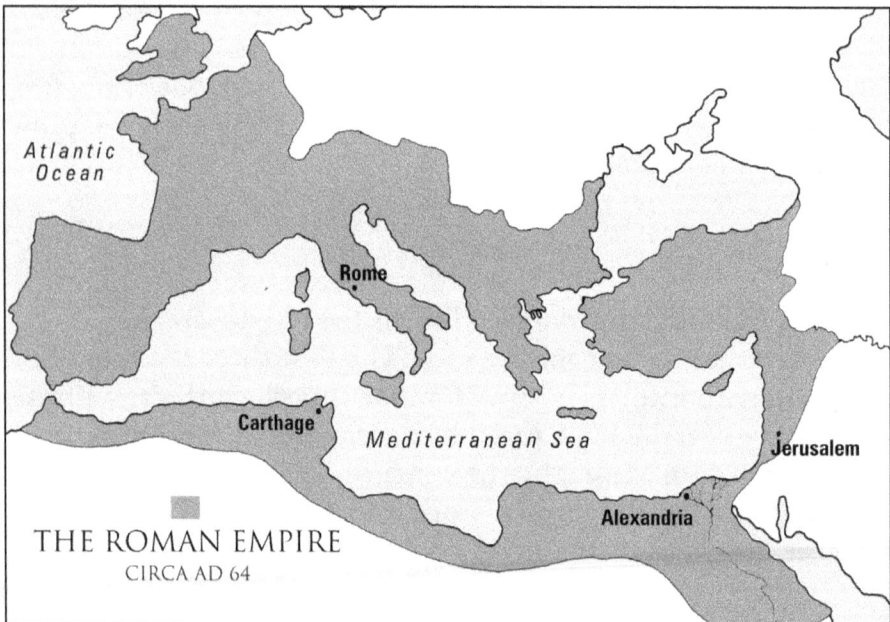

Atlantic
Ocean

Rome

Carthage

Mediterranean Sea

Jerusalem

Alexandria

THE ROMAN EMPIRE
CIRCA AD 64

Remembering

In the past three sessions, we have found the early Christian community in a world of persecution. They tried to remain faithful under difficult circumstances, but the ongoing distress caused problems within the church. Throughout our study, the fabric of the church has been torn and ripped, yet a thread of hope has remained—hope that the faithful will respond to God and restore their relationships with one another.

The letter of Jude is an urgent message to a community in danger. The church was in dissension, facing potential destruction. False teachers polluted the church with wrong ideas, and many church members were persuaded by the deceiving words of these teachers.

Our text is from the end of Jude's letter. In his final thoughts, Jude restates his argument against the wrongdoers and makes a passionate appeal to the church. Preceding his appeal, Jude warned readers of those who pervert the gospel. These false teachers promoted a gospel that freed the saved to live as they pleased, without worry over consequences. Obviously, this belief was tempting, swaying some toward a shallow, self-serving faith.

Faith becomes stagnant and sometimes polluted when we allow worldly pleasures and petty talk to distract us. We may lose sight of God, and our relationships are often weakened. Jude offers advice on how to grow in faith and remain in God's love.

Studying

With references to fallen angels, Sodom and Gomorrah, waterless clouds blown around by the wind, and stars wandering in deepest darkness, the letter of Jude is intense. It could be likened to receiving a brief e-mail written in ALL CAPS! It's an urgent message—one that can quickly catch your attention. Jude hoped the church would hear his argument and put forth a genuine response.

Although Jude, brother of James, claims authorship in the letter, there is some speculation that another person wrote the letter, using the name and authority of Jude. However, the former argument carries more weight by the fact that the author was knowledgeable and familiar with Jewish literature and traditions—therefore supporting Jude as the actual author.

Also at issue is whether Jude was the brother of Jesus. Most scholars who point to Jude as the author believe he was the brother of James and Jesus. Jude (a shortened form of Judas) was a common name in the early church, but the only brothers with the names Jude and James mentioned in the New Testament are the brothers of Jesus (Mt 13:55; Mk 6:3). If we accept *this* Jude as the author, then likely he wrote mid-first century.

Obviously, the recipients of Jude's letter were in a troubling situation. Following his greeting, Jude mentions that his motives for writing have changed. Apparently, he had become more aware of the dissension and destruction "false teachers" were spreading in the community. So with strong words, Jude speaks against these evildoers and demands that the church hold strong to their faith.

To whom was Jude writing? Was it to one particular church or to the entire Christian community? Little information in the letter points to a specific audience. Perhaps Jude hoped many Christians facing similar problems would read this letter. For example, the recipients of 2 Peter faced circumstances similar to the situation in which the recipients of Jude found themselves (Mills, 1320). Certainly, the problems concerning Jude were universal to Christians in the early church.

The identity of the "scoffers" and "worldly people" mentioned in the text is not definite. Several groups could be identified as the troublemakers. Most would agree that the evidence of false teaching and the successful manipulation within the church suggest that the opposing side was predominately Gentile. The author's focus on Jewish history and tradition also supports the claim that non-Jewish groups were corrupting the "faith that was once for all entrusted to the saints" (Jude 3).

These false teachers proclaimed a perverted doctrine: "They understand the gospel of freedom in Christ to relieve a Christian of ethical responsibilities, an understanding that 'perverts grace'" (Watson, 475). They believed that, once saved, they were free to

Paul, too, struggled with this attitude in some of his congregations, especially in Corinth. There, followers of means felt privileged enough to exclude poorer members from the table of fellowship by eating early and often. In that instance, Paul admonished the wealthy by pointing out how their self-aggrandizing actions were detrimental to the larger body of faith. In the end, Paul instructed them to put the community before their own needs.

satisfy their desires and wants. It was a tempting and distracting message, to say the least.

Interestingly, members of this group were not necessarily outsiders to the faith community. In fact, the author describes them eating jovially alongside the Christians at the love feasts (Jude 12). Because they had woven themselves carefully into the fabric of the community, it is not surprising that the author urged the church to be attentive to the Holy Spirit and assertive in their actions. The opposition had become a serious threat, and the church needed to respond.

Understanding

The closing of Jude's letter not only reiterates his main argument, but also contains a passionate appeal to the church at large. The appeal begins with a reminder of the apostles' prediction that the activity of scoffers would signify the end of days (Jude 17-18). Jude's urgency is understandable since he, along with the rest of the early church, believed that the end of time was near.

The author continues to describe the problematic group, who focused on worldly things and caused divisions. Persecution notwithstanding, the Christian community was further separated by those "devoid of the Spirit" (Jude 19). Everything about these corrupt people stood in opposition to the loving work of God.

After spending the majority of the letter focusing on these slanderers, Jude finally turns to the people of genuine faith. It's as if he says, "Now, here's what *you* can do!" Duane Watson points out that the first four exhortations, or appeals, are things the Christians could do for themselves; the last three exhort the faithful to deal with those who have fallen prey to the false teachers (497). Notice the responsibility is both inward and outward.

Mercy was considered a divine characteristic. God's mercy for Israel is well documented in ancient Jewish literature. Usually, mercy is described as part of God's "steadfast love" for God's people. Even in the stories of Adam and Eve, Cain and Abel, David and Bathsheba, as well as other stories of disobedience, God's judgment is always coupled with mercy. Little wonder Jesus told Peter and the other disciples to forgive not once or even seven times but to mercifully offer forgiveness seventy times seven.

Verse 20 invokes an image of the Christian community coming together in spirit and action, turning their focus away from the persecutors and toward a holy, unpolluted faith. The second appeal is for prayer, and the third is for them to remain consumed in God's love. The final exhortation concerns hope for eternal life. Jude reminded the faithful that the end was coming soon and that the mercy of Christ would bring them life everlasting. Apparently, some wavered or doubted their faith. Jude called Christians to show them mercy. Even those individuals entangled in the web of the false teachers could be saved if the Christians were willing to help them.

The practices offered in Jude are faithful actions the church found significant in building and maturing Christian character. The early church knew that intentional practice was the only means for God to work through our lives. Transformation was and is a gift of God's love, but our will has to be reigned in. Not one of us moves to faith while simultaneously progressing from self-absorbed to kingdom-oriented. That change is a process, and it requires faithful practice along the way. Jude encourages, even admonishes, these followers to form their faith by practicing it.

The early church developed spiritual practices for its initiates and candidates for baptism. Many took these practices so seriously that candidates would have to work with a mentor in the faith for at least a year, and in some instances three years, before they could be baptized.

The final appeal is for the church to offer mercy to the persecutors while always being careful not to be "touched" by their sinful "clothing." Jude was optimistic that God could transform this church, especially if the Christian community would quickly respond to his appeal.

What About Me?

• *Build one another up in faith.* We must support each other. It is our responsibility as a family of faith to help each other through difficult times and even seek opportunities to reach out to the "scoffers."

• *Prayer changes us.* An ongoing conversation with God strengthens the relationship. When we actively listen, we mature in our faith and are moved to act.

• *Confront one another in love.* In love, we must respond to those who divide and wrongly persuade. Confrontation motivated out of love and concern can bring unity and reconciliation.

• *Have mercy!* Because Jesus Christ is merciful, we must offer mercy to those who have strayed from God. It is easy to fall into sinful habits, especially when distracted by selfish desires. Our gift of grace may be their opportunity for restoration to the family of God.

Resources

Watson E. Mills, "Jude," *The Mercer Commentary on the Bible,* ed. Watson E. Mills et al. (Macon GA: Mercer University Press, 1995).

Duane F. Watson, "The Letter of Jude," *The New Interpreter's Bible,* vol. 12 (Nashville: Abingdon Press, 1998).

SPEAKING OF PERSECUTION

Jude 17-23

Introduction

Jude is a special name to me. My uncle Julian, nicknamed "Jude," was a gracious and forgiving believer who "sparkled on me" when I was growing up. Jude actually is a shortened form of the name Judas. Tradition holds that this Judas was the brother of Jesus (Mt 13:55).

While much of the letter has an ominous tone of warning, the letter's basic context is positive and hopeful. The aim is to help believers become faithful, redemptive members of the community of faith. Note the affirmation with which Jude begins and concludes the letter. I like Eugene Peterson's paraphrase of the first and last paragraphs. He offers a word of hope and love, plus an invitation to trust God more than anything:
I, Jude, am a slave to Jesus Christ and brother to James, writing 7to those loved by God the Father, called and kept safe by Jesus Christ. Relax! Everything is going to be all right; rest, everything's coming together; open your hearts, love is on the way! (1-3)

And now to him who can keep you on your feet, standing tall in his bright presence, fresh and celebrating—to our one God, our only Savior, through Jesus Christ, our Master, be glory, majesty, strength and rule before all time, and now, and to the end of all time. Yes. (*The Message*, [Colorado Springs: NavPress, 2002] 24-25)

Dag Hammarskjøld, the Swedish believer and diplomat, wrote a benedictory prayer near the untimely end of his life, similar to Jude's, expressing gratitude and continuing commitment to God: "For all that has been: Thanks! To all that will be: Yes!" (*Markings*

[New York: Alfred A. Knopf, 1965], 64). Such a prayer seems to complement the dual purpose of this letter, which is to relax, trust God, and receive the blessing that comes only from God.

An excellent follow-up to last week's session from Titus concerning personal behavior, Jude has three major concerns. Let us explore those concerns.

I. A Warning about Disruptive People in the Church, 17-19.

One purpose of this letter was to warn Christians about libertines flaunting their freedom and filling the church with errant teaching. While they posed as serious believers, Peterson paraphrases, "They treat faith like a joke, and make a religion of their own whims and lusts" (18).

These mockers continue to divide the church. They have heard the good news that Christ has freed us from the law, but they violate that sacred liberty by rowdy unlawfulness and infidelity. They are self-centered, not God-centered.

Remembering Jesus' and Paul's constant battle with Pharisees and those overly bound by the law helps put Jude's message into its appropriate context. Pharisees were good people, but they were rigid and judgmental, caustic and condemning. Even today, it seems that some are too narrow and others too broad. In other words, some have the window of law stuck shut so that no fresh air and freedom of the spirit of God can enter. Others have the window stuck open so that the stability and necessary structure of God's household is threatened.

Jude 16 describes the character of the dividers: grumblers, malcontents, lustful, prideful, arrogant, and manipulative through flattery. The word "grumblers" is precisely the word used of the people of Israel who left Egypt grumbling (*goggustes*) at Moses about their hardships. Their focus was on themselves and their comfort, not on God and the needs of others.

The problem is not simply that such behavior for believers is unacceptable—although it certainly is. The point is not to be critical and judgmental of others or self-righteous. The primary issue here is division of the kind that polarizes the community of faith. This disunity then undermines the worship of God, the spreading of the good news, and the ministry to hurting, needy people.

Jude's insightful diagnosis of the problem hits the bull's eye: these prideful grumblers are "devoid of the Spirit" (19). He calls people to pay attention to the spirit of God and to their own spiritual development as they relate to God as Creator, Christ, and Holy Spirit. Jude calls us away from self-satisfaction or self-absorption and toward growth in grace and graciousness.

II. A Call for Spiritual Growth in Our Character, 20-21.

Jude offers a corresponding list of spiritual qualities he urges us to cultivate so that we may develop mature faith:
(1) Establish a holy faith.
(2) Live in constant prayer in the Holy Spirit.
(3) Live out of the center of God's love.
(4) Look forward to God's mercy, which leads to eternal life.

Consider last week's calling from Paul through Titus about the cycle of God's grace. This week, we have a choice to live out Christlike love, regardless of vocation. Jude suggests:
• On what are we founding and focusing our lives? Jude asks for focus on faith. Faith is precisely what Moses' followers grumbled about: they wanted security more than faith. Faith was too scary and unpredictable for them.
• Prayer in the Spirit is centering one's life in the prayer of Jesus: "Not my will but yours, O God, be done." This kind of prayer has more to do with listening to God and relishing a relationship with God than with advising God or besieging God with requests.
• Living in the love of God suggests we cannot build our lives upon love of self. Human love can be selfish, egotistical, grasping, and controlling. God's love is freeing, enriching, and it calls us to pass that love onto others.
• Looking forward to "God's mercy, which leads us to eternal life" reminds us again of last week's session. We are called to partnership in passing God's mercy onto others, just as we have received grace that we didn't deserve.

Notice that Jude introduces himself as "the brother of James," but "the slave of Jesus" (1). Obedience to the loving God seems the key to spiritual growth. The problem with both the libertines and the Pharisees is that neither wants to trust or obey God. Rather than worship God in spirit and truth, they project who they are onto God.

A major question regarding our spiritual growth is what we do with the gifts God gives us—mercy, grace, forgiveness, second chances, material blessings, energy, health. Do we hoard God's gifts or pass them on? Our growth as spiritual people depends upon our being to others what God is to us: a giver of grace.

III. A Word Concerning How to Relate to the Dividers, 22-23.

One of the worst things we can do in the church is to harbor a "them and us" attitude concerning those outside the church. God calls us to face the evil in ourselves as well as the evil in others. While it is much easier to point out the evil in others, it is necessary to allow the Scripture to become a mirror that reflects that not all evil is outside of us; much is indeed inside. We are sinners. Remember last week? We heard Paul bemoaning his own sin: "I can will what is right, but I cannot do it. I do not do the good I want, but the evil I do not want is what I do" (Rom 7:18-19).

Dividers have "them and us" attitudes, but even those who don't approve of the dividers can practice "them and us" as well. We can escalate divisions while trying to quell them if we don't learn grace from the God of Jesus. How do we approach the problem of such divisions?

Perhaps Jude learned from watching Jesus face division, or from Paul, who once persecuted believers and eventually became an apostle, a leading writer, and a "good news-er" in the community of the faith he once attacked. Paul might say to us, "Do for your divisive people what God did through Barnabas for me." Pass grace on! Our Christian call is to include, not exclude, such people, whether the problem is their belief or behavior. We are charged to invite them back into the fellowship of God's church if at all possible.

Last week, Paul advised Titus about what to do if reclaiming dividers was impossible. Jude says the same thing in a different way: "Go easy on those who hesitate in the faith. Go after those who take the wrong way. Be tender with sinners, but not soft of sin. The sin itself stinks to high heaven" (23).

We have heard, "Hate the sin and love the sinner." Is that being soft on sin? I don't think so. Does it condone the sin to love the sinner any more than God's forgiveness condones sin when God forgives? Is it possible to separate sin and the sinner? C. S. Lewis helped me see that I do it all the time: "For a long time I used to think this was a silly, straw-splitting distinction: how can you hate what a man does and not hate the man? But years later it occurred to me that there was one man to whom I had been doing this all my life—myself. However much I might dislike my own cowardice or conceit or greed, I went on loving myself" (*Mere Christianity* [New York: The Macmillan Company, 1943], 90).

In addressing divisions, (1) be as clear as possible about what you believe, (2) listen respectfully to those who differ in viewpoints or behaviors, and (3) stay in touch with God and each other as we try to share and develop our faith without human creeds or coercion. May God help us learn to practice as well as receive both grace and forgiveness. May God help us learn the grace of talking with each other rather than about each other.

Notes

Notes